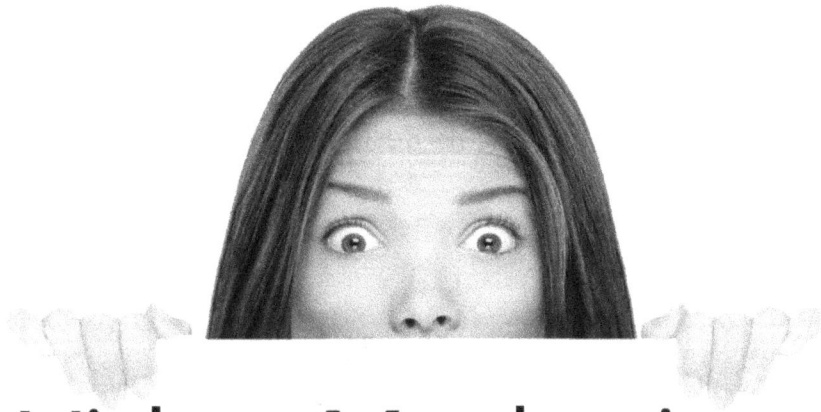

# Video Marketing for Entrepreneurs

Workbook

## From Selfie to Network TV
## + Bonus Tips

Red Carpet
ACADEMY

Author

Co-Author

*Anita Miranda*   *Samantha Leiter*

Video Marketing for Entrepreneurs Workbook
From Selfie to Network TV + Bonus Tips

Living Disabled Publishing
Publication Date: 2016
First Edition, 2016
Printed in USA
10987654321

Paperback Color Edition - ISBN: 978-0692609378
Paperback Black and White Edition - ISBN: 978-0692609392
Workbook Color Edition - ISBN: 978-0692611920
Workbook Black and White Edition - ISBN: 978-0692610060

**Author:** - Anita Miranda
**Co-author:** - Samantha Leiter
**Edited & Illustrated by:** - Samantha Leiter
**Design, Layout, & Graphics Design:** - Samantha Leiter, Anita Miranda & Barb Anderson
**Cover Design:** - Barb Anderson

Proceeds benefits Circle Of Helping Hands, a 501(c)(3) #04-3821284

Contact the Author:
Anita Miranda: transform@anitamiranda.com
www.AnitaMiranda.com

# Acknowledgments

Anita Miranda with Circle of Helping Hands, a 501(c)(3) (COHH) is grateful for the contributors and the participants of the very first Red Carpet Academy Workshop held in San Diego, CA. Also to Felena Hanson and her staff who offered her amazing Hera Hub co-working space to set our stage.

Proceeds from Red Carpet Academy media kit benefits COHH's mission, to assist Veterans, Women and their Children by providing Advocacy, Career Skills and Community Involvement.

## Keynote Speakers:

Felena Hanson

Jenn Kaye

Angela Chee

Natalia Robert

Anita Miranda

## Bonus Tips Contributors:

Holly Kolman

Barb Anderson

Anne McColl

Giselle Fox

Skyler McCurine, copywriting

## Participants:

Laurie Itkin

Gail Kraft

Holly Kolman

Kaliani Cynthia Hupper

Skyler McCurine

Jenny D. Beato

Susan Atooli

Anne-Marie Diggle Rabago

Elena-Lene Gravgaard

Ellen Scott Grable

Karen D. L. Kramer

## Media PRO and More Staff Volunteers:

Samantha Leiter

Carrie Brooks

Mathew Hupper

Mike from Chicago (our homeless man who I never got his last name)

# COHH

## Veterans, Women & Their Children

Circle of Helping Hands Inc. (COHH), a 501(c)(3) non-profit corporation, tax ID# 04-3821284

Circle of Helping Hands, (COHH) 501(c)(3) is a federal program funded by services, grants, donations and contributions. The organization is headquartered and operated by volunteers of the community whose mission is to advocate for Veterans, Women and their children.

## WHO WE ARE:

We assist in applying for eligible social benefits for those who find themselves in a "Now What" moment due to divorce, layoff, health issues, etc.

We specialize in helping individuals who are seeking benefits from military, Medicare, unemployment, Social Security or/and state assistance.

We also foster the establishment, growth, expansion, and pay it forward of businesses through our community with internships, mentors, and various services.

COHH is a grass roots training organization whose vision is to help locally, train locally, mentor locally, hire locally, to plant the seed by simultaneously *"Paying It Forward."*

# Table Of Contents

**Poised**    **Polished**    **Professional**

# Red Carpet Academy Foreword

It's a new day; it's a new quarter and it's going to be the best one yet, I can feel it. Public speaking is known to be one of our greatest "fears." Now, let's add a couple of photographers, videographers and a live microphone? This would rank pretty high in our fear factor wouldn't you agree? I know how it feels to be in front and behind the camera. And both are not easy feats. I am not a celebrity or a spokes model nor a natural beauty. I wanted to create a production set to help women be seen, be heard and be beautiful. What we at Red Carpet Academy provide are the tools, experience and practicum to be camera ready.

Red Carpet Academy is your first step to preparing for your camera ready, anytime anywhere opportunities. This workshop is a smart investment for you and your company's future. You will feel confident in front of the camera, behind the camera, and implement Red Carpet strategies to grow your company along with new friends and colleagues to help you achieve it.

We have assembled a great line-up of industry experts, ready to share their practical tools, relevant topics and useful strategies for your video needs. Expect to be amazed and entertained while energizing your mind, maximizing your skills and empowering you to feel and look beautiful no matter what shape and size.

Red Carpet Academy appreciates the generous support of many wonderful supporters, associations, interns, mentors and our life experiences that make this event possible. I am especially grateful to my volunteers and for the support of our experts. I hope you enjoy what we have produced and have some fun.

Thank you so much for coming and entrusting us with your most precious commodity, You!

Truly Honored,

*Anita Miranda and Team*

# 1ˢᵗ Annual Red Carpet Academy

# Red Carpet Academy Workshop
## PRESENTS
# Keynote Speakers

Jenn Kaye - Communications Strategist

Felena Hanson - Marketing Strategist

Natalia Robert - Photography Specialist

Angela Chee - Media Specialist

Anita Miranda - Video Strategist

# About Our Speakers

## Jenn Kaye - Head-On Communications & Touch With Intention

Jenn is an internationally recognized communication and lifestyle expert, as well as an author and media personality. Principal of Head-On Communications LLC, she is known for helping her clients and audiences align their businesses, brand and lifestyle with their unique and authentic expression.

With a background in languages (Japanese, Spanish, French & a little Russian), wellness, entertainment and personal transformation, Jenn has a special way of translating your message into an experience that not only creates greater connection with your market and audience, it reminds you of your own magnificence and contribution in the world.

Having facilitated a diversity of world class groups for over 20 years, such as the U.S. Government's Department of Defense; including the Marines, Air Force, and Army; Capital One, The Atlantis Hotel, Royal Caribbean Cruise Lines and Kaiser Permanente Health Systems, she continues to passionately coach and consult with leaders who are ready to live their life head-on and are committed to making a difference.

## Felena Hanson - Hera Hub

Felena is a long-time entrepreneur and marketing maven. Her 20-year career has spanned from technology start-ups to digital marketing agencies. Some of her former clients include DirecTV, Epson, CNN, and Union Bank. Before becoming an entrepreneur she was Director of Marketing for a venture-backed San Diego Internet company that sold to America Online in 2003.

As Felena launched her first business, Perspective Marketing, she found her passion for supporting other female entrepreneurs through leadership roles with several professional women's organizations, including Ladies Who Launch and Women's Global Network.

Hera Hub, is a spa-inspired shared workspace and community for female entrepreneurs. This as-needed, flexible work and meeting space provides a productive environment for growing businesses. Hera Hub members have access to a professional space to meet with clients and to connect and collaborate with like-minded business owners, thus giving them the support they need to be prosperous. The business supports hundreds of freelancers, entrepreneurs, and nonprofits in over 16 industry segments.

After building three successful locations, she franchised the business and is expanding across the United States. Her next goal is to support over 20,000 women in the launch and growth of their business by 2020.

Felena is passionate about education, earning her Bachelor's degree in Marketing from the University of San Diego and her MBA from California State University Dominguez Hills. She taught Marketing and Entrepreneurship at the Fashion Institute of Design & Merchandising and at California State University Dominguez Hills for the MBA online program for eight years.

Felena and Hera Hub have been featured in Inc. Magazine, the BBC News, Forbes, and the New York Times. She has been nominated for numerous small business awards and has been rewarded for her efforts by winning the 2012 "Women Business Owner of the Year" award and the 2014 "Women Advocate of the Year" award from the San Diego chapter of the National Organization of Women Business Owners. In 2014 she also won the "Small Business Champion of the Year" award from the San Diego Small Business Administration.

## Natalia Robert - Full Circle Images

Natalia has been photographing life for over 15 years and is bringing her unique eye to spaces and businesses all over Southern California. Her world travels, love of the outdoors, and fun energy blend perfectly for a memorable photo session that is tailor-made to each client. Her years in architecture and graphic arts, meanwhile, bring a keen design eye to all final images. While Natalia is always happy behind a camera, she especially enjoys photographing beautiful homes, as well as collaborating with fellow local business owners to refine their branding images.

## Angela Chee - Zen Media Inc.

Angela Chee is a Host, Writer, Speaker and Founder of Zen Media Inc., a media training and consulting company. She helps companies and individuals grow their business and brand by more effectively sharing their product, service and message with the media. With more than 15 years of experience in the broadcast industry, Angela is an award-winning journalist who has worked as an Anchor/Reporter for KNBC-TV and KCBS/KCAL-TV in Los Angeles, Fox 6 in San Diego, E! Entertainment Television, and hosted shows for HGTV (Home and Garden Television), The International Channel, Channel One News and helped launch Entertainment Tonight China. Merging her traditional media background with her social media influence she is also the Founder of The Zen Mom.com, an informative and inspirational website with the mission to empower through wisdom, inspiration and laughter and The Zen Mom TV. She has also been a contributor for various sites including Lifetime Moms, Momversation, Patch, and Mom Logic.

## Anita Miranda - Miranda's Creatives, LLC & Circle of Helping Hands

Anita Miranda is a media and self-help entrepreneur with many years of experience helping women become prepared for on-camera appearances and showing them how to look and act their best while the camera is pointed at them. She recently developed Red Carpet Academy for those who are preparing to be in front of, or want to be behind the camera, shooting their own videos in the convenience of their own home. She also penned her autobiography: *Anita Miranda, PTSD and Me: How Bill Clinton Got Me Out of Bed*.

She is the Founder and Creative Director of Miranda's Creatives, LLC, a company that prepares women how to present themselves in the best possible light when they are on camera, mostly geared towards corporate and business professionals who need to give interviews, present materials, or have to be filmed for other reasons. Every client receives the VIP experience.

Anita Miranda has a Master's Degree in Education and a Bachelor's Degree in Business Administration with decades of experience in the field. She is also the founder and current president of the Circle of Helping Hands, a nonprofit advocacy group and skill set training center. She is a retired, disabled veteran of the Navy. Anita lives in Scottsdale, AZ.

# Introduction

This workbook is designed in connection with the DVD's, Audio CD's, and Paperback editions. We tailored each segment to be more than just theory; it's actual practicum. You may start at any section and travel through the chapters as needed. Many participants say that they set aside a few hours a day in order to watch, read, and utilize the workbook. Learning a new skill set may be overwhelming. Remember, this media kit was designed to assist you at your pace; anytime and anywhere.

A Red Carpet Academy Certification logo is available to those who pass the online quiz. By earning the RCA certification, you will demonstrate to booking agents that you are qualified and "Media Ready."

Enjoy.

*Anita Miranda and Team*

# In Front of the Camera:
## Techniques and Tips For Appearing on Video
### _Simplify your Message_

**Honest - Meaningful - What makes YOU different**

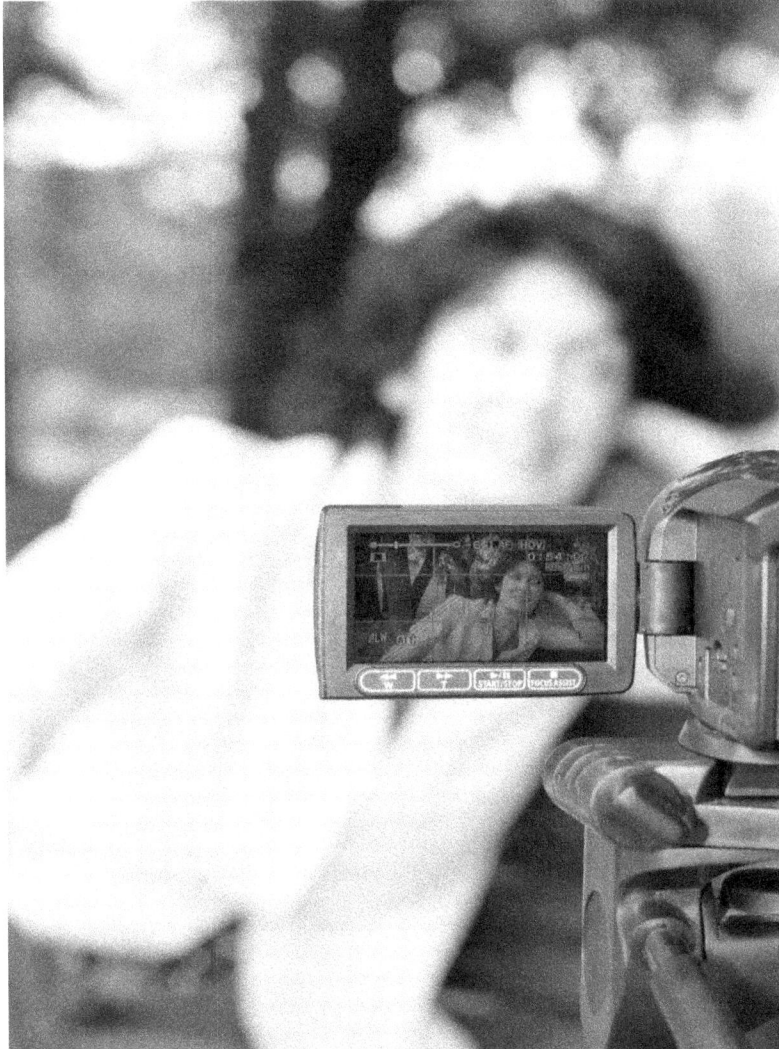

**Video is _NOT_ forgiving!**

- _Cannot Photoshop_
- _Cannot hide behind props_
- _Changes can be costly_

- _Professional video production can be expensive_
- _And the number one reason?_
- _Video is personal_

_"A MOVIE CAMERA IS LIKE HAVING SOMEONE YOU HAVE A CRUSH ON WATCHING YOU FROM AFAR - YOU PRETEND IT'S NOT THERE."_
_- TOM STOPPARD_

# What is my Selfie Style?

**1. Angle techniques:**

Notes:

**2. My three best smiles are:**

1.
2.
3.

Notes:

**3. Indoor lighting locations:**

Notes:

**4. Outdoor lighting locations:**

Notes:

**5. Take lots of selfies and choose the very best ones.**

Notes:

# Jenn Kaye

Jenn Kaye is a Master Communicator, Language Expert and Keynote Speaker whose contagious enthusiasm adds a refreshing spark to everyday challenges. Through her corporate trainings, facilitation and high-impact keynote presentations, Jenn has emerged as a relevant voice and progressive thought leader on the art of communication.

Jenn teaches progressive companies how to embrace change, foster collaboration and accelerate performance.  Her inspiring style educates and encourages audiences to become more authentic, resilient and engaged as leaders. With a background in languages, Jenn's special talent for tying results-based performance back to purposeful language choice is unmatched.

Beyond her professional success, Jenn has never let her story define her. Having overcome a life-threatening illness and recovered from a head-on collision, she is a true advocate for the authentic expression of the human spirit.

Engaging, real and insightful, Jenn delivers intentional and customized, high-content programs for your audiences with bite-size wisdom they can implement immediately.

FEATURED
SHEKNOWS  FEMINA  SELF

# MASTER THE LANGUAGE OF COMMUNICATION™

### Speaking

Engaging, humorous and insightful, Jenn delivers high-content programs for your leadership conference, corporate event or sales meeting with bite-size wisdom they can implement immediately.

### Training

Jenn's interactive and engaging programs will educate your leaders how to create the clarity and communication they need to have more influence and impact every day.

### Coaching

Investing in your ongoing professional development is key to staying resilient in today's ever-changing landscape. Work one-on-one with Jenn to identify your strengths and learn how to use language to get results

"We have an especially tough audience of franchise owners for our international cafes. They are hard to please and usually close-minded. I've never seen them engage as much as they did at our national conference with Jenn's keynote "Upping Your Customer Experience Game." She not only had them interacting and energized, she spoke our language so fluently, she sounded like she could be part of our company. I feel confident they will be able to implement what they learned in new and lasting ways."

-Shawnon Bellah, V.P. of Domestic & International Operations, Nestlé TollHouse® Café

"Jenn Kaye's ability to listen is like nothing I've ever experienced. She seems to capture the essence of who you are, and helps you find just the right way to say exactly what you want to convey, if only you'd known how to say it! I've helped thousands of leaders from Ivy League Institutions for over 20 years, and while I teach interpersonal communication, Jenn breathes it through her very DNA."

- Roxi Bahar Hewertson, CEO Highland Consulting Group

480.442.5433 | Linkedin.com/in/jennkaye | Jenn@JennKaye.com

# 10 Tips to Engage Any Audience

**1. Own the Space**
   Notes:

**2. Smile**
   Notes:

**3. Let Go of Perfection**
   Notes:

**4. Be Real**
   Notes:

**5. Be Ready for the Unexpected**
   Notes:

**6. Love Your Voice**
   Notes:

**7. Speak From Your Heart, Not Your Head**
   Notes:

**8. Use Your Whole Body to Communicate**
   Notes:

**9. Practice the Power of the Pause**
   Notes:

**10. Make Your Message About Them**
   Notes:

# Tips for What to Eat (and NOT to Eat)
## Before Going On-set or Onstage:

Before you ever go on set or onstage, use your critical thinking skills beforehand. Your energy is directly reflected by the food you eat, so as a general rule of thumb eat foods that give you energy and avoid foods that weigh you down or distract you from being fully present mentally, emotionally or physically.

**There are some that may ask the question, "To eat or not to eat?"**
   Notes:

**What foods to avoid:**
   Notes:

**What foods to consider:**

**1. Eat light**
   Light in calories, light in weight.
   Notes:

**2. Snacking within the hour.**
   If you must snack within an hour of speaking or going on camera, keep your 'eat light' mantra in mind and consider some of the following:
   Notes:

**3. Drink plenty of water.**
   Water makes up over 90% of our body and brain. Staying hydrated will keep your mood uplifted and your brain fresh!
   Notes:

# Green Screen

**1**. **What Are the Pros & Cons of Using a Green Screen?**
   Notes:


**2. Lighting Techniques:**
   Notes:

**3. Be the Director:  Know Your Vocabulary**
   Notes:


**4. To Mic or Not to Mic?**
   Notes:


**5. Necessary Equipment:**
   Notes:

**6. Using Multiple Cameras:**
   Notes:

**7. Audio Techniques:**
   Notes:

**8. How to Use a Professional Teleprompter:**
   Notes:

**9. Is It Necessary to Memorize Your Script?**
   Notes:

**10. What Must I Have in My "Impromptu" Bag for Opportunities?**
   Notes:

## 11. What Does My Hair Style Say About Me?

Notes:

## 12. To Accessorize or Not To Accessorize?

Notes:

## 13. What is My Color and Style Saying About Me?

Notes:

# Behind The Camera:
## How To Create A Spectacular Video

Notes:

> "FILMMAKING IS INCREDIBLE INTROSPECTIVE. IT FORCES YOU TO SORT OF EXAMINE YOURSELF IN NEW WAYS."
> - DREW GODDARD

1. **What Are the 5 Basic Shot Types?**
   Notes:

2. **How to Frame Correctly and Why?**
   Notes:

3. **Is High Definition Worth the Extra Cost?**
   Notes:

4. **What are the Differences Between Print and Web Resolution?**
   Notes:

5. **How to Stage Your Background to Convey Your Message:**
   Notes:

6. **Lighting: Indoors Versus Outdoors:**
   Notes:

**7. How to Create Your Own Teleprompter: YouTube has excellent samples.**
   Notes:



**8. Always Test Your Equipment:**
   Notes:



**9. What is your Back up Plan Regarding Equipment?**
   Notes:



**10. Green Screen and Editing**
   Notes:



**11. Check the Audio Through Your Camera & Computer**
   Notes:

# Full Circle Images
## Photography by NATALIA ROBERT

email: natalia@fcisandiego.com

website: www.fcisandiego.com

FB: www.facebook.com/fullcircleimages

Instagram: @fullcircleimages

Twitter: @fullcircle_sd

phone: 858-255-0855

# Staging

By:
Natalia Robert

Full Circle Images

Full-circle-images.com
Facebook.com/fullcircleimages
fullcircle_sd

Notes:

# Lighting

## Natural

## or

## Artificial?

*Photo provided by Full Circle Images*

Notes:

# Turn on all available lights

*Photo provided by Full Circle Images*

Notes:

# Flood the room with natural light

*Photo provided by Full Circle Images*

Notes:

# Be aware of shadows

*Photo provided by Full Circle Images*

Notes:

# Perspective

From above

*Photo provided by Full Circle Images*

Notes:

Straight on

Leading lines

*Photo provided by Full Circle Images*

Notes:

# Pops of color add life

*Photo provided by Full Circle Images*

Notes:

## Final tips:

### Check your frame.
Check alignments and awkward angles

### Test shoot before you shoot.
Take test shots before going for the real thing

### Always have back-ups.
Batteries, SD cards, cameras, plans

### Know your resolutions.
Low resolution -  72 ppi
High resolution -  300 ppi

### Know when you need professional help.
A professional can save you time and money

*Photo provided by Full Circle Images*

Notes:

# Red Carpet Extravaganza

"PEOPLE WILL STARE. MAKE IT WORTH THEIR WHILE."
- HARRY WINSTON

# Zen Media inc.

## Need Media Exposure? Not Sure Where To Start? Don't Know What To Say Or How To Say It?

The media landscape is changing. The integration of traditional and new media gives you more channels than ever to get noticed and to reach your customers. While this is a great opportunity, it can also be a little overwhelming, unless you're prepared.

**Zen Media Inc.** will give you the skills and confidence you need to propel your business to the next level. From pitch to message to interview, our workshops, one on one training, and customized consulting services will help you grow your business and your brand. You will be able to more effectively share your product, service, and message with the media.

## Media Training and Consulting Services:

**Story Development and Pitch Training**
**On Camera Media Training**
**On Air Talent Coaching**
**Media Placements**
**Image Consulting**
**Spokesperson/Voiceover Talent**
**Website Videos**

Owner **Angela Chee** has worked with entrepreneurs, authors, bloggers, reporters, hosts and organizations. With more than 15 years in the broadcast industry, she is an award-winning journalist who has worked as an Anchor, Host, and Reporter for NBC and CBS in Los Angeles and Fox in San Diego, E! Entertainment Television, HGTV (Home and Garden Television) and helped launch Entertainment Tonight China for Paramount Pictures.

She's heard thousands of media pitches and interviewed prominent politicians, executives, entrepreneurs, officials, and celebrities. Before her news career, Angela worked in advertising and public relations giving her insight into all aspects of media. Today she has merged her traditional media background with her social media influence to create The Zen Mom. com. With her broad media experience, she knows how to package a story, communicate effectively, and get you the results you want.

*"Angela was able to help our organizations understand how the media works, making us feel comfortable, confident and ready for any situation."*
**Orange County Chamber of Commerce**

*"I have thoroughly enjoyed working with Angela. She is not only a fabulous spokesperson and a natural on camera, but very supportive of helping local businesses. It is a pleasure to recommend Angela to anyone looking to boost their business through media consulting or media placement!"*
**-Danielle Podlesny, Owner-Munchkin Minders**

## Go to ZenMediaInc.com to get FREE Media Training Tips!

angela@zenmediainc.com • (310) 489-6134  www.facebook.com/AngelaCheeTV  @angela_chee and @thezenmom

# *Media Training Tips*

Zen Media inc.

## The Interview

Have a media interview, but nervous about what to say or how to say it? Here are a few Zen tips to make sure you are confident and prepared.

1. **Before your interview, make sure you define your key messages**. These are the most important points you want to get across during your interview. Make a list of some brief messages that can be stated in 15 seconds or less. Know what you want to communicate and convey them in "sound bites."

2. **Be brief and stay on point**. Remember your key messages and know that reporters may only use one or two eight second "sound bites." Make your words count. If there is only one message, say it several times in different ways.

3. **Listen to the question before responding**. Don't get distracted. Make sure you know what question you are answering.

4. **Stay in control of the interview**. Make sure you present your key messages in the beginning, even if the interviewer doesn't ask the question.

5. **Image is important**. Dress for the audience, but always look professional and polished. Bright solid colors look best. If wearing a dark suit, accent with colorful blouse or tie. Do not wear anything distracting, striped, loud prints, or jewelry.

Notes:

# The Pitch

Whether you get news coverage depends on how you pitch your story. While there is no one "right" way to convey your message, there are ways to help make sure you are heard and get on the air.

1. **Make sure you have the right contact**. You don't want to leave a message on a general voicemail box. Find someone you can pitch or get the correct e-mail address. It can be a reporter, an assignment editor, booker, or a producer.

2. **Don't just send a press release.** Attach the press release for additional details, but make sure you write a specific short pitch at the top.

3. **Know your hook.** Create a tie-in with your service or product with a newsworthy story. Ask yourself, why would anyone care about the story? What makes the story interesting? Why would a producer/editor want this story in their show or column? Find a legitimate connection to a hot topic and you can increase your chances of getting coverage.

4. **Provide resources.** Make the reporters/producers job easy. It's not enough to give a story idea; you also need to help them tell the story. Offer to supply the reporter with background information, interviews, sources, and video/photo opportunities. Be specific.

5. **Know the right time and show to pitch.** What type of story is it? Who does it appeal to? A light feature may do better on the weekends when the media outlet is short on stories. Harder news stories are for the evening news. Mid-day news may be good for health, senior, and women's issues. Morning News is good for live interviews.

Notes:

1.  **How & When to Strike a Pose:**

Notes:

2.  **How to Win the Media Over:**

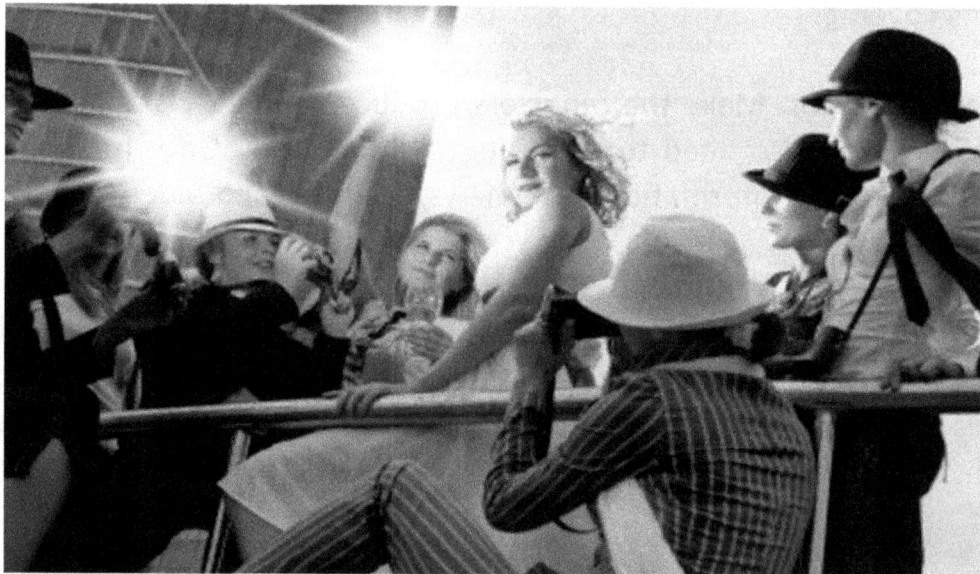

*Where to Use Videos*

- Press Releases
- Social Media Platforms
- Landing, Sales and Website
- Print Media
- Broadcast Media

*Be Ready...*

- Prepare
- Practice
- Persuade

Notes:

## 3. We Help Those Who are Camera Shy
First impressions make the difference; being camera ready is the difference.

Notes:

4. **Camera Angles That Make Me Look Good!**
   Notes:

5. **Why is it important to Practice Your Natural Smile Every Time!**
   Notes:

6. **How to POP on the Red Carpet with Some Vibrant Colors!**
   Notes:

7. **How to Maximize the Red Carpet Interview:**
   Notes:

8. **Ready, Set, Get that Sound Bite (15 and 30 Seconds):**
   Notes:

9. **Volunteer to Tape a Testimonial and the Benefits:**
   Notes:

10. **Hit Your Mark, Whether You Are Going Solo or Within a Group:**
    Notes:

11. **How to Convey Confidence as an Industry Expert!**
    Notes:

## 12. How to Flash a Natural Smile Every Time:

Notes:

# HERA HUB
## WORKSPACE FOR WOMEN

**Felena Hanson, Founder of Hera Hub**

Felena is a long-time entrepreneur and marketing maven. Her latest venture, Hera Hub, is a spa-inspired shared workspace for female entrepreneurs. This as-needed, flexible work and meeting space provides a *productive* environment for women who primarily work from home. Hera Hub members have access to a *professional* space to meet with clients and to connect and collaborate with like-minded business owners, thus giving them the support they need to be *prosperous*. Cost-effective monthly membership options are suited for freelancers, independent consultants, entrepreneurs, nonprofits, and authors.

Hera Hub is much more than just a shared workspace; it's a community of like-minded entrepreneurial women who find the additional resources, such as special classes, workshops, and one-on-one support essential for their business growth. Hera Hub has two San Diego locations with a third in Carlsbad. The company is also available for franchising.

Felena is passionate about education, earning her Bachelor's degree in Marketing from the University of San Diego and her MBA from California State University Dominguez Hills. She taught Marketing and Entrepreneurship at the Fashion Institute of Design & Merchandising and at California State University Dominguez Hills for the MBA online program for eight years. Felena was most recently rewarded for community efforts, as she was awarded the "Women Business Owner of the Year Award" by the local chapter of the National Organization of Women Business Owners.

# Hera Hub
## 619-889-7852
## HeraHub.com

# Customize Your Sound Bite

1. Your elevator pitch should include things such as your name and business, but more importantly, it needs to focus on benefits. "What's in it for me? What are you going to do for me?"

2. An analogy can help give people an idea of what your business is like by using a comparison to something in completely outside of your industry that is easily recognizable. So whenever you are doing something a little different, using an analogy can really help you audience understand it.

3. If you are a founder or a creator, mention it. Too many people glaze over this fairly important detail that the audience should know.

4. Focus on what makes you different. There are likely a lot of people who do the same basic thing you do, so what separates you from them? How do you stand out?

5. Be sure to end with a zinger. Have a tagline that the audience will easily remember.

6. It is much easier to get perspective from other people.  Have someone you know, but don't know well, help you work on your pitch and find what stands out about your business.

7. Don't try to be the same or similar to your competitors. You want to stand out.

8. Make sure that your message leaves an impact. It needs to be meaningful to your target audience.

9. Make it short and sweet. You only have a short period of time to impress your audience.

10. What you want to think about as well is "how does this come out on video" and "how are you building a connection with your audience immediately."

# Bonus Material

> *"I'VE ALWAYS HAD THE UTMOST RESPECT AND AWE OF WHAT THE LENS CAN DO AND WHAT A DIRECTOR CAN DO WITH JUST A CAMERA MOVE."*
> *- MATTHEW GRAY GUBLER*

# Anita Miranda
### SPEAKER • AUTHOR • VETERAN • ENTREPRENEUR

As seen & heard on

SONORAN LIVING LIVE | SAN DIEGO LIVING | Latino Perspectives | ENGLISH | VOICE AMERICA | blogtalkradio

*Lights! Camera! Action!*

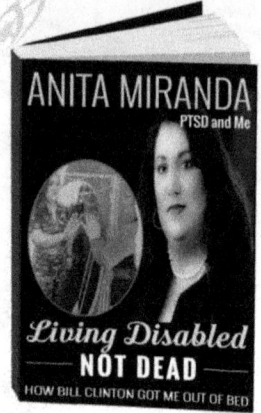

ANITA MIRANDA
PTSD and Me

*Living Disabled*
NOT DEAD
HOW BILL CLINTON GOT ME OUT OF BED

Anita never imagined that one day she would be a Director, Videographer, Advocate & Author, now she is living her dream! It wasn't always that way. It would have been easy to let insecurity, hard knocks and past life experiences defeat her. From ward of the court to a retired disabled Veteran, Anita made a choice to earn a Master's degree and be the creator of her own destiny!

Anita tackeled her own fear of being in front and behind the camera to share her own journey and skills to others so they too can create their own spotlight.

# Video Equipment Recommendations

## Using a Smartphone as a Camera

If you are using a smartphone as a camera, you'll want a simple, but effective tripod like the following.

PEMOTech® Mini Tripod Universal Octopus Style Mount

A simple, but effective tabletop tripod for all Apple and Android phones.

http://tiny.cc/brgk7x

ChargerCity MegaGrab2 Easy-Adjust Smartphone Holder Mount & 360° Swivel Adjustment Selfie Video Recording Camera Tripod Adapter

This adapter is for those who already have a tripod or are getting a regular one, but want to be able to use it for their phone. It works for both the Iphone and for most Android phones.

http://tiny.cc/evgk7x

# Cameras

One of the most important pieces of equipment is your camera. If you would like something of a higher caliber than your smartphone, here are some options:

### Kodak PlayTouch Video Camera

This camera records in 1080p HD and is compatible with 32 GB SD cards. It allows you to see more details and accurate colors in low light. It has an external microphone jack that lets you record in stereo.

http://tiny.cc/a5gk7x

### Canon EOS Rebel T3i Digital Camera SLR Kit

A full kit with a wonderful, quality video camera. It includes lenses, a 16 GB SD card, flash, a carrying case, and more.

http://tiny.cc/i8gk7x

RedCarpetAcademy.org

# Tripods

A good tripod can be just as important as a good camera.

Ravelli APLT2 50" Light Weight Aluminum Tripod with Bag

A good, solid tripod that extends to a height of 49 inches.

http://tiny.cc/0dhk7x

# Lighting

A set's lighting has a strong effect on the final look of the shot, so you want to be sure to have a great lighting set-up.

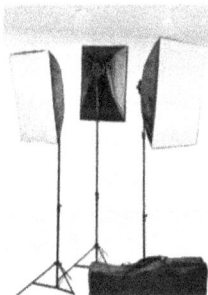

Fancierstudio 3000 Watt Digital Video Continuous Softbox Lighting Kit

A nice quality lighting kit perfect for a 3-point lighting set-up. The lights come with softboxes, a great addition for video.

http://tiny.cc/nghk7x

# Microphones

You want to have audio that sounds nice and clear, so you will want an external microphone.

### ATian SGC-698 Photography Interview MIC Microphone

A nice, consumer quality mic that will pick up audio better than your camera's internal mic.

http://tiny.cc/hkhk7x

### Audio-Technica ATR-3350 Lavalier Omnidirectional Condenser Microphone

A good quality omni-directional lavalier. It is mono, not stereo, so keep that in mind.

http://tiny.cc/jthk7x

# SD Cards

When using a digital camera, you'll need an sd card with a a fair amount of space, as you'll need it to record video.

Transcend 32 GB Class 10 SDHC Flash Memory Card

A quick and efficient SD card with palnty of space for all of your video needs. As a class 10 card, it will easily be able to capture your video with no problems. It is usable with any camera that can use a class 10 SD card.

http://tiny.cc/z1hk7x

# Editing Programs

There are plenty of quality video editing programs out there. If you only plan on creating the occasional video, programs such as Movie Maker and IMovie will work just fine. However, if you plan on creating a lot of high-quality videos, it would be wise to look into a program like Adobe Premier or Final Cut Pro.

# Your Equipment on Hand

## Plus Extras

List the equipment you currently have here. If you plan on doing video in a professional capacity, you should have *at least* a camera, an SD card that is at least 16 GB and is a class 10 or higher, a tripod, a set of three lights (preferably with soft boxes), an external microphone compatible with your camera, and a computer with video editing software. Other items that can be helpful to have included are lavaliere microphones, a clapboard and extension cords.

1.

2.

3.

4.

5.

6.

7.

8.

9.

10.

# *What Equipment Do You Need?*

## Your Wish List

**Is there any equipment that you're missing? Or is there anything that you want a better version of for a beginner level? What items would be helpful?**

1.
2.
3.
4.
5.

**Are you planning on advancing your skills to the intermediate level? What items would you need?**

1.
2.
3.
4.
5.

**What equipment do you need for a professional level? What items would be helpful?**

1.
2.
3.
4.
5.

# Vocabulary

**Audio Check** - A test of the volume of your voice; you'll typically be asked to count to ten by an audio engineer.

**B-roll** - Video footage that shows action without sound.

**Bust Shot** - Chest-to-Head shot framed above the elbows.

**Chroma Key** - The process of putting a virtual background into a video during post-production. Used in tandem with green screen.

**Close-up (CU)** - A close view of an actor or an object, featuring details isolated from their surroundings. A close-up of an actor typically shows only his head.

**Cue** - A signal (as a word, phrase, or bit of stage business) to a performer to begin a specific speech or action

**Cue Card** - A card held beside a camera for a television broadcaster to read from while appearing as if looking into the camera.

**Elevator Pitch** – A brief and effective sales speech.

**EPK** - Electronic Press Kit. Includes video and stills to promote a product or service.

**Establishing Shot** - A camera shot, usually at long range, that identifies or establishes the location of a scene.

**Extreme Close-up (XCU)** - A very close view of an actor or an object featuring minute details. An extreme close-up of an actor typically shows only his eyes or part of his face.

**Extreme Long Shot (XLS**) - A panoramic view of a film scene, photographed from a great distance

**Eyeline** - Where a subject appears to be looking, typically into the camera or screen left/right.

**Frame** – Look for horizontal and vertical lines in the frame (e.g. the horizon, poles, etc). Make sure the horizontals are level, and the verticals are straight up and down.

**Full Shot** - A long shot that includes the human body in full within the frame

**Green Screen** - The backdrop against which an interview or action is filmed that allows a computerized or virtual background to be inserted during post-production.

**Headroom, Looking Room, & Leading Room** - These terms refer to the amount of room in the frame that is strategically left empty.

**Head Shot** - Just a talking head. Rarely used in live TV because people move too much.

**Jump Cut** - An abrupt transition from one scene or clip to another.

**Lavaliere Mic** - A small microphone that clips to your shirt or jacket. Often called a lav.

**Live Streaming** - Live video content delivered over the Internet.

**Live Shot -** A live broadcast of a reporter speaking to the camera, typically done from the field.

**Long Shot (LS) -** A shot that shows a fairly broad view of a subject within its setting. A long shot of an actor typically includes his entire body and much of his surroundings.

**Mark -** Your spot for the scene will be marked on the floor, usually in an X or T formation with some glaring piece of colored tape.

**Medium Shot (MS) -** A relatively close shot that shows part of a person or object in some detail. A medium shot of an actor typically shows his body from the knees or waist up.

**Package -** A video story edited together that typically includes interview soundbites, b-roll footage, a recorded voice over (track), and a stand-up from a reporter; usually between one to three minutes long.

**Rule of Thirds -** This rule divides the frame into nine sections, as in the first frame below. Points (or lines) of interest should occur at 1/3 or 2/3 of the way up (or across) the frame, rather than in the center.

**Selfie –** A picture one takes of one's self, usually with a smartphone or tablet.

**Sit-down Interview -** A recorded interview that a reporter may edit for soundbites or broadcast in its entirety.

**Soundbite -** An edited clip of a recorded interview, typically 8-30 seconds long.

**"Standby on the set"** - This means "attention" and "quiet" on the set. The command is given 15-30 seconds before rolling tape.

**Stand-up -** a video clip of a reporter talking directly to the camera, from the field. Also called piece-to-camera.

**Teleprompter -** A machine that displays text directly under the camera lens to prompt the person speaking; also called an autocue.

**Track -** A narrator or reporter's voice recorded on tape and edited together with b-roll; "to track" is to read and record your script. Also called VO or voice over.

**Two-shot -** A medium shot featuring two actors

**Wide Shot -** Normally the full setting, stage edge-to-stage edge, top to bottom within a frame.

# Red Carpet Academy Workshop
## PHOTO GALLERY

*Before*

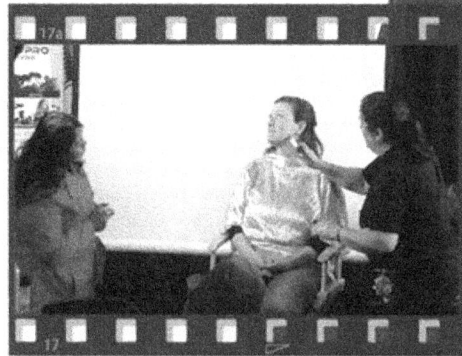

# Red Carpet Academy Workshop
## PHOTO GALLERY

# Red Carpet Academy Workshop
## PHOTO GALLERY

# Red Carpet Academy Workshop
## PHOTO GALLERY

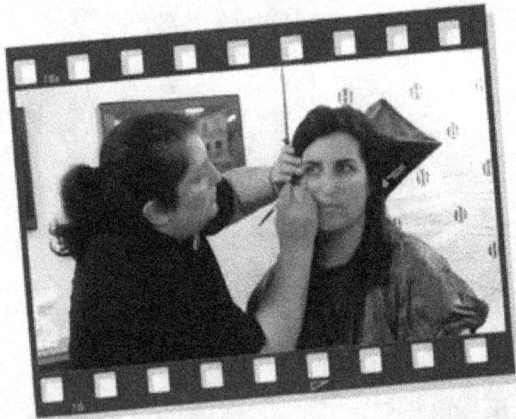

# Red Carpet Academy Workshop
## PHOTO GALLERY

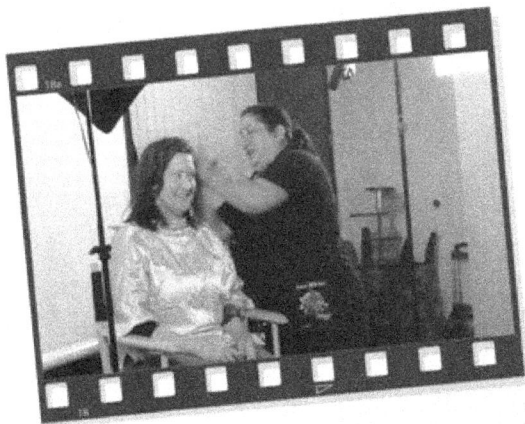

# Red Carpet Academy Workshop
## PHOTO GALLERY
### After

# Certification

For certification purposes - please go to http://tiny.cc/RedCarpetAcademy, or scan the QR code below, and click on Certification.

Then complete the quiz. You will have two attempts to pass with 80% or higher. If you do not pass on the second attempt, you can retake the quiz after 30 days. In the meantime, please review the book, workbook, and videos. Or, you can request a personal coaching session with a Red Carpet Academy instructor for a nominal fee. We ensure your success and quality of our certification. We look forward to your graduation pictorial, video, and to a prosperous future.

Upon graduation, you will receive the official Red Carpet Academy Seal to demonstrate your skill set. You may place on digital or printed materials.

*Anita Miranda and Team*

# Sample Model Release

In consideration of my engagement as a model, upon the terms herewith stated, I hereby give to [photographer] _____, his/her heirs, legal representatives and assigns, those for whom the photographer is acting, and those acting with his/her authority and permission:

a) the unrestricted right and permission to copyright and use, re-use, publish, and republish photographic portraits or pictures of me or in which I may be included intact or in part, composite or distorted in character or form, without restriction as to changes or transformations in conjunction with my own or a fictitious name, or reproduction hereof in color or otherwise, made through any and all media now or hereafter known for illustration, art, promotion, advertising, trade, or any other purpose whatsoever.

b) I also permit the use of any printed material in connection therewith.

c) I hereby relinquish any right that I may have to examine or approve the completed product or products or the advertising copy or printed matter that may be used in conjunction therewith or the use to which it may be applied.

d) I hereby release, discharge and agree to save harmless [photographer], his/her heirs, legal representatives or assigns, and all persons functioning under his/her permission or authority, or those for whom he/she is functioning, from any liability by virtue of any blurring, distortion, alteration, optical illusion, or use in composite form whether intentional or otherwise, that may occur or be produced in the taking of said picture or in any subsequent processing thereof, as well as any publication thereof, including without limitation any claims for libel or invasion of privacy.

e) I hereby affirm that I am over the age of majority and have the right to contract in my own name. I have read the above authorization, release and agreement, prior to its execution; I fully understand the contents thereof. This agreement shall be binding upon me and my heirs, legal representatives and assigns.


Print Name: _____

Signed:_____

Dated: _____

Address:_____

City:_____

State/Zip:_____

Phone:_____

Email: _____

# Lighting Diagrams

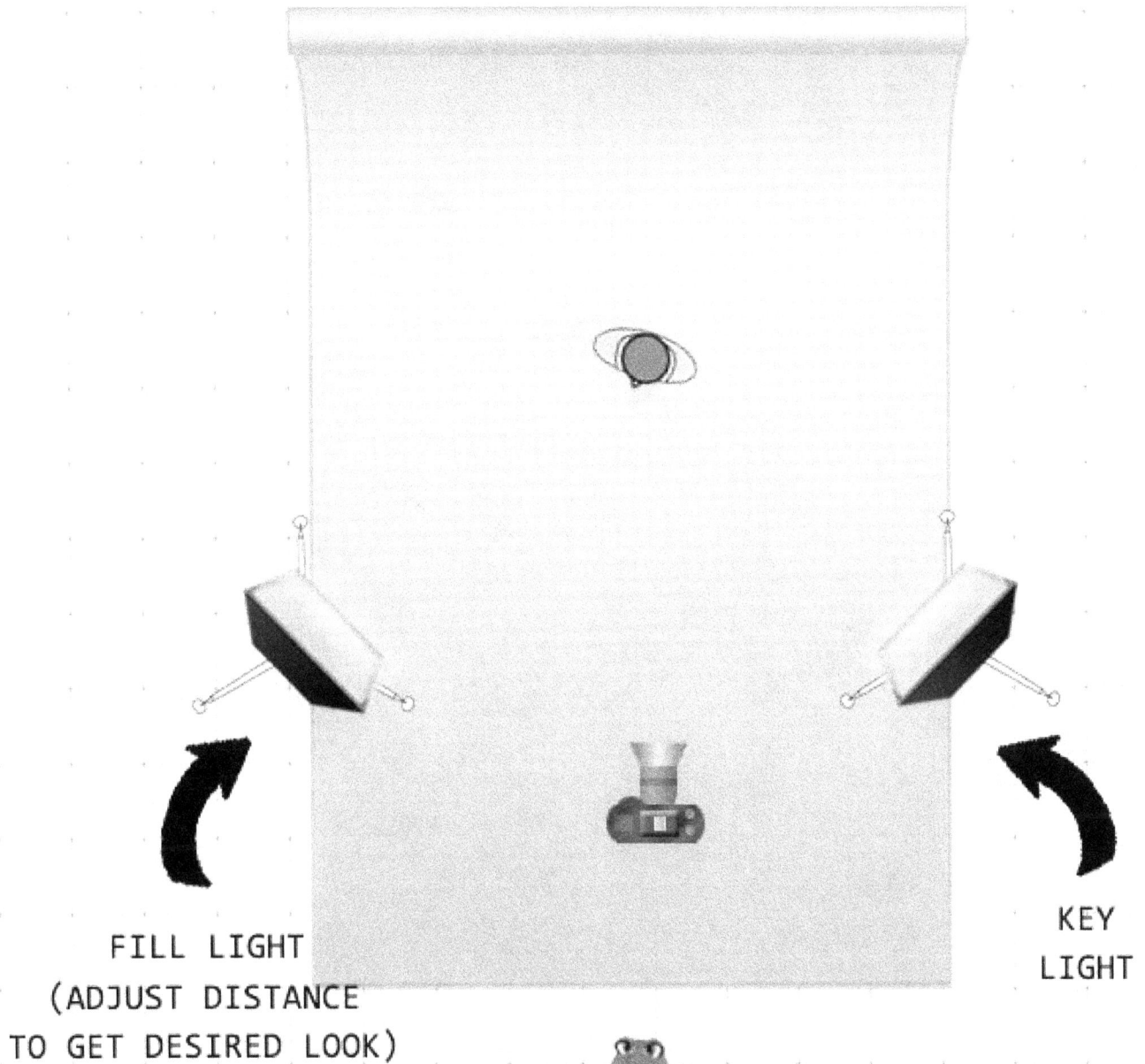

FILL LIGHT
(ADJUST DISTANCE
TO GET DESIRED LOOK)

KEY
LIGHT

MediaPRO
andMore

IMAGES COURTESY OF OUR FRIENDS AT LIGHTINGDIAGRAMS.COM

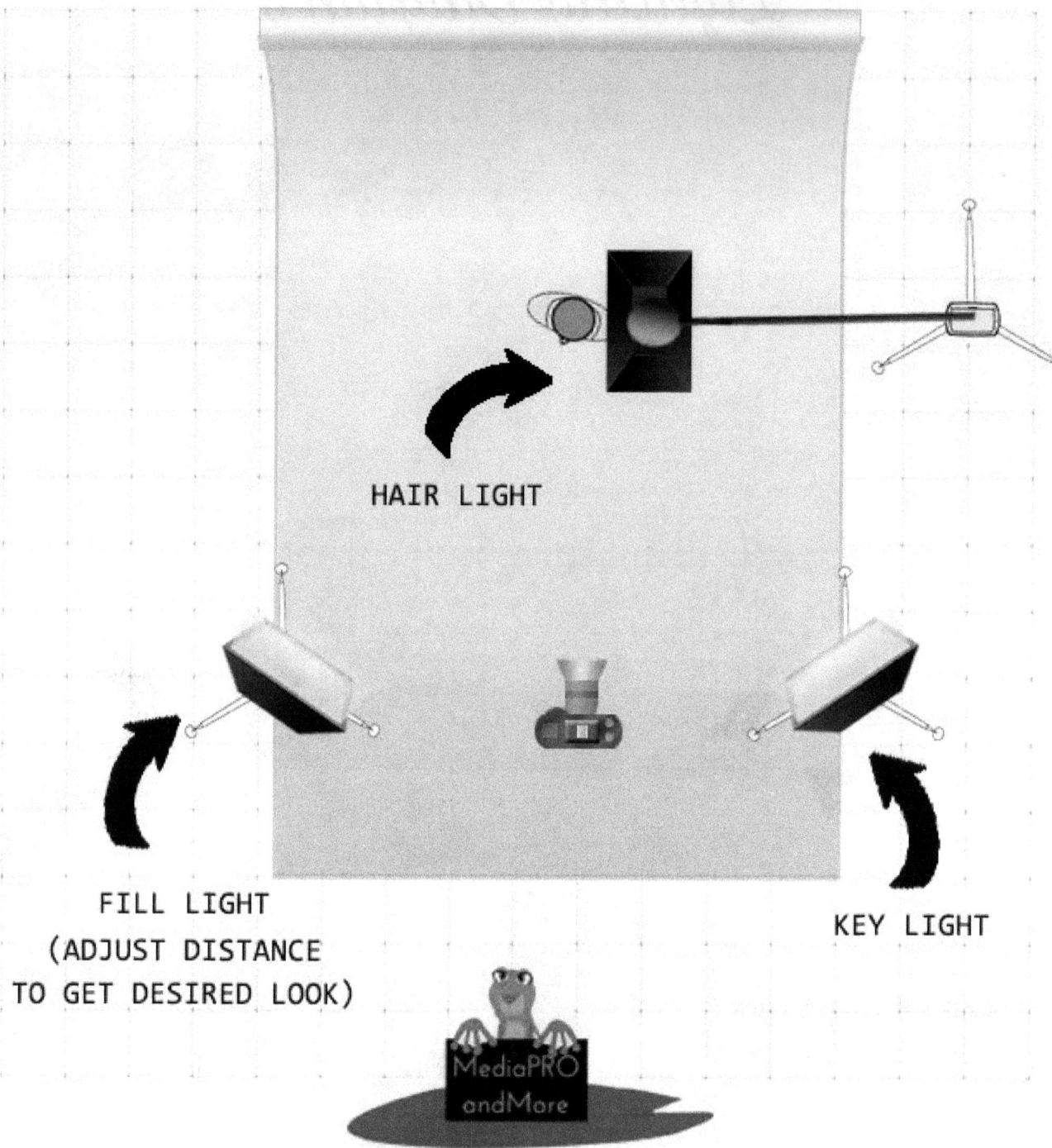

HAIR LIGHT

FILL LIGHT
(ADJUST DISTANCE
TO GET DESIRED LOOK)

KEY LIGHT

IMAGES COURTESY OF OUR FRIENDS AT LIGHTINGDIAGRAMS.COM

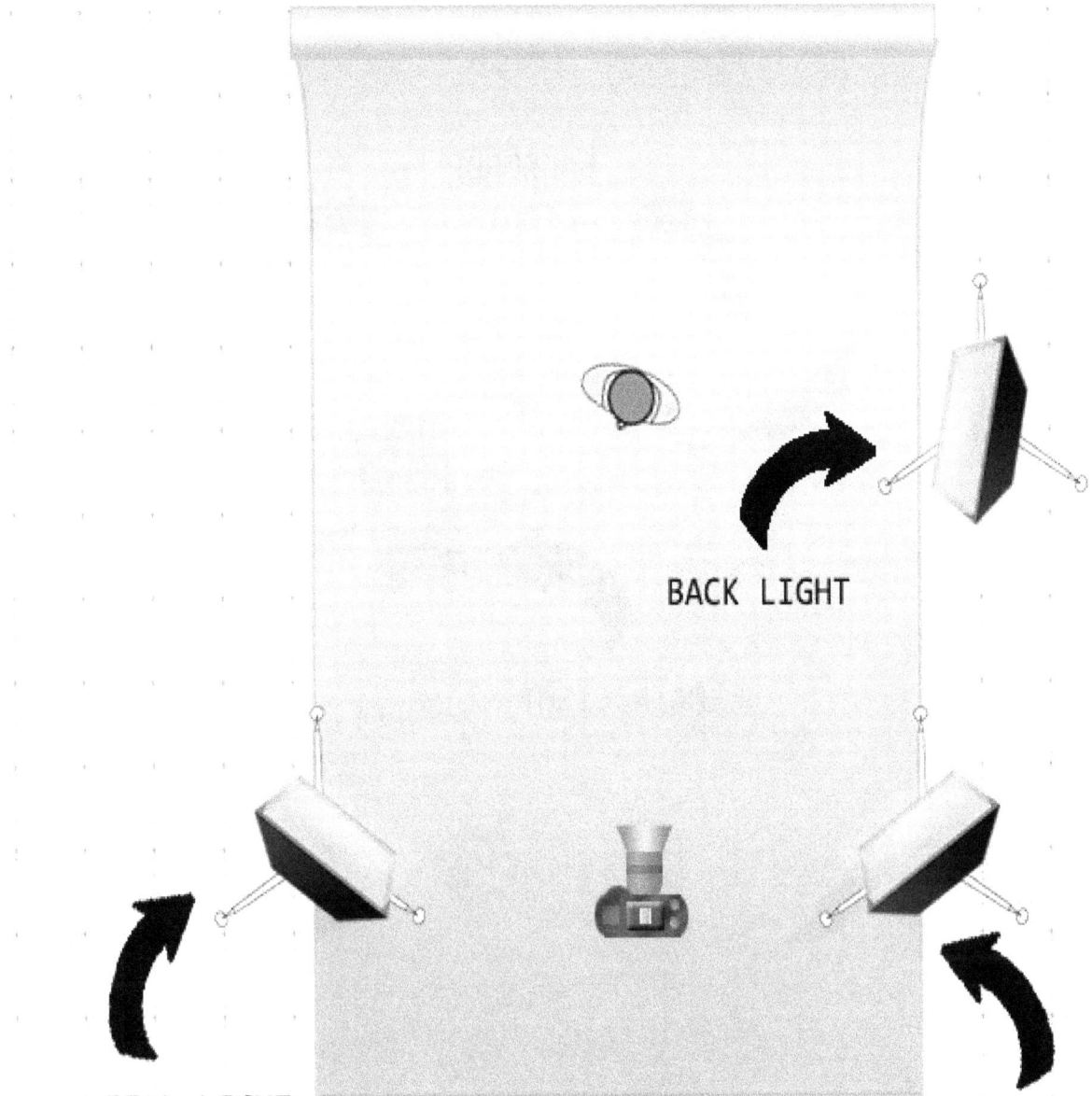

BACK LIGHT

FILL LIGHT
(ADJUST DISTANCE
TO GET DESIRED LOOK)

KEY
LIGHT

MediaPRO
andMore

IMAGES COURTESY OF OUR FRIENDS AT LIGHTINGDIAGRAMS.COM

BACKDROP
LIGHTS

HAIR LIGHT

FILL LIGHT
(50% POWER)

KEY
LIGHT

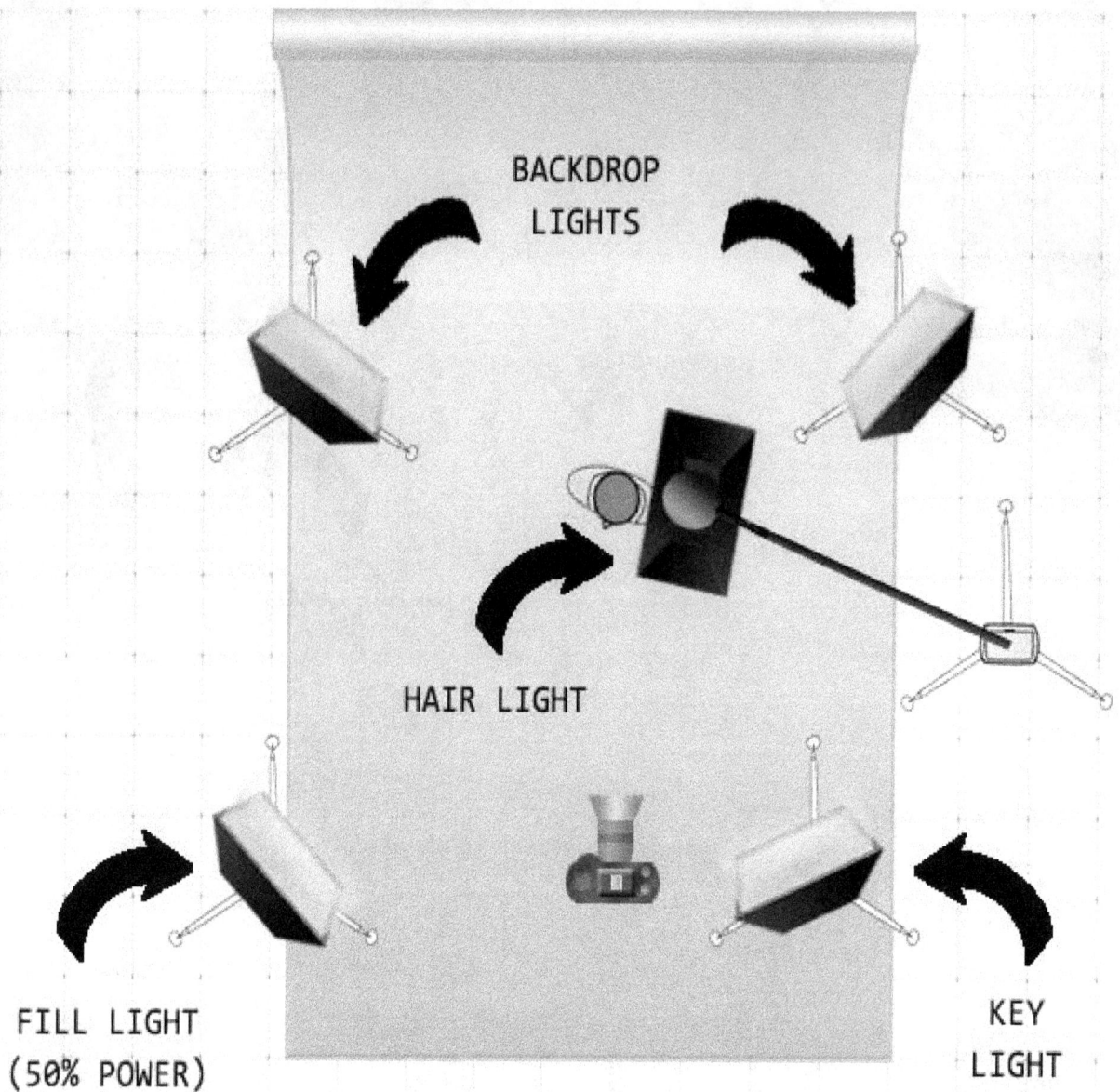

IMAGES COURTESY OF OUR FRIENDS AT LIGHTINGDIAGRAMS.COM

# 50 Great Ways To Use Your Video

MediaPRO andMore

## Customer Reference Videos
1. Video Customer Testimonials
2. Video Success Stories
3. Video Case Study
4. Man-in-the-Street Interviews
5. Customer Presentations

## Product and Service Promotions
6. Product Presentations
7. Product Demonstrations
8. Product Reviews
9. How To
10. Subject Matter Experts
11. Product Comparisons

## Corporate Videos
12. Corporate Overview
13. Executive Presentations
14. Staff Presentations
15. Corporate Facilities
16. CEO Updates
17. Corporate Communications

## Training and Support Videos
18. Training Videos
19. Instructional Videos
20. Expert Videos
21. Just-in-Time Learning
22. Post Sale Support Videos
23. Maintenance Videos

## Internal Communications Videos
24. Webinars
25. Event/Conference /Trade Show
26. Employee Orientation
27. Health, Legal & Safety Issues

## Advertising, Marketing and Promotion
28. Commercials
29. Viral Video
30. Email Video
31. Infomercials
32. Content Marketing
33. Landing Pages and Micro Sites

## PR Support and Community Relations
34. Video Press Releases
35. PR Support Materials
36. Community Relations Video

## Event Video
37. Event Presentation Video
38. Round Table Sessions
39. Q & A Expert Sessions
40. Highlights or Red Carpet Video

## Other Uses of Video
41. Recruitment Videos
42. Video Blogs (Vlogs)
43. In Store Video
44. Company Lobby / Waiting Room
45. Mobile Video
46. Market Research
47. Website FAQ Video
48. Video White Paper
49. Video Magazine
50. Author Bios and Book Promotion

## IMPRESS & ENGAGE WITH VIDEO
## CALL TODAY FOR A PERSONALIZED QUOTE

RedCarpetAcademy.org

# Sample Storyboard

Intro_____

_____

_____            _____

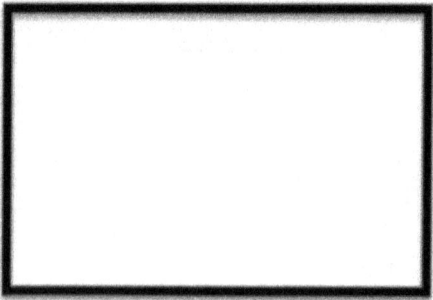

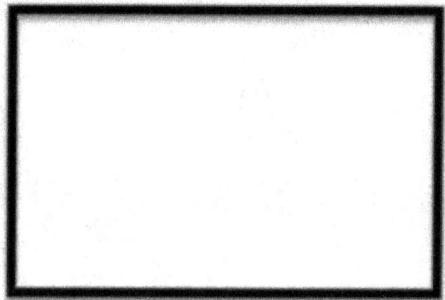

_____            _____

_____            _____

_____            _____

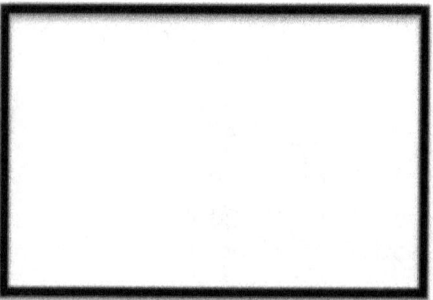

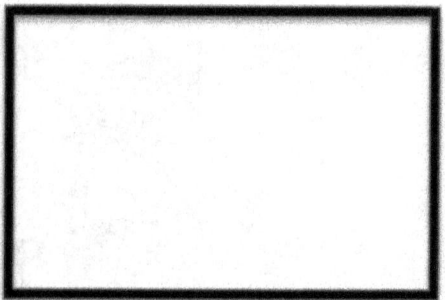

_____            Outro_____

_____            _____

_____            _____

# Shot List Sample

Date: _____

Date of Shoot: _____

Name of Client: _____

Company Name: _____

Signed Letter of Release? _____

Video Style: Action, Romantic, Clean, Typography

Type of Video: Sells, Informs, About Me, Welcome, Trailer

Time Keeper: 30. 45. 60. 90+

Director: _____

To be filled out by videographers:

Takes _____ Best Take _____

Takes _____ Best Take _____

Takes _____ Best Take _____

Signature: _____

Paid / Deposit _____

Creative Session: _____

Time: _____

How Many People: _____

Names: _____

Music: Provided by Client or Media PRO

Music Title: _____

(No copy write infringement)

Green Screen: YES or NO

Choose: Natural, White or Black drop (Circle)

Approved: _____

Website: www.
Facebook: www.Facebook.com/
Telephone number:

Testimonials: YES/NO    How Many: _____

## Video Production

### Scene 1              Name:

Subject Matter

Script Provided?                    Make-up Provided?

Who and what does your Company do or provide? 15 second elevator speech

Why your company?

Call to action either giveaways, free offer, and          Deliverable: 30 days
how to contact you:

# Congratulations!

You have completed the *Video Marketing Tips for Entrepreneurs Workbook* of the Red Carpet Academy!

Now what?

Professional videos are required when separating your brand from your competition. This kit provides In Front of the Camera, Behind the Camera, and Red Carpet Ready tips.

Hiring a professional video team can be costly. Most production companies charge based on the hours from start to finish. As a Red Carpet Academy graduate, you will be every videographer's dream of being *"Camera Ready;"* saving you both valuable time and money.

Need great videos or one on one coaching?

> Contact Media PRO and More
> http://www.anitamiranda.com/contact-us/ for your complimentary creative session.
>
> Custom video production services are available.
>
> Call or email: 877-605-6389 or quote@redcarpetacademy.org

# Other Books By Anita Miranda

http://tiny.cc/nsd2yx
to get your copy

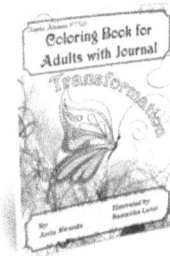

## Beacon
Publishing House

Nana Knows PTSD: Paperback, Hardcover, Workbook,
DVD, Audio & Other Publications Available.
Other Titles Coming Soon.